YOUNG, DUMB, AND FULL OF POEMS

Hasti is a poet and writer living in South East London. A member of the inaugural Southbank New Poets Collective and the Ledbury Poetry Critics, they are the recipient of the 2023 White Review Poet's Prize and the 2022 Queen Mary Wasafiri New Writing Prize for Poetry. Hasti has also co-written short sci-fi film *DIGGING*, produced by Film4. Hasti hosts open mic and poetry night Fresh Lip, and its sister show for Montez Press Radio, *Fresh Air*. This is their first book.

First published in 2025 by Little Betty, an imprint of Bad Betty Press
Cobden Place, Cobden Chambers, Nottingham NG1 2ED

badbettypress.com

Copyright © Hasti 2025

Hasti has asserted their right to be identified as the author of this work in accordance with Section 77 of the Copyright, Designs and Patents Act of 1988.

PB ISBN: 978-1-913268-82-4
EPUB ISBN: 978-1-913268-83-1

A CIP record of this book is available from the British Library.

Book design by Amy Acre

young, dumb, and full of poems

HASTI

LITTLE BETTY

CONTENTS

Poet as Cyborg Pornstar	7
Poem as Zereshk Pollo	8
Mixed White/Asian And/Or Multiple Other (Specify):	9
Rostam in the 21st Century	10
Ghazal	11
Our Honeymoon with the Machine	12
Poem in the Form of a Fax Machine	13
Pay Enough And You Too Can Bathe In Crude Oil	14
Annihilation	15
Neuroplastic	16
VR	18
I have fallen from my dream of progress	19
Farsi Word for Orange	20
Love Letter with Ansible	23
Gol-e Yakh	24
Killer	25
All of the Light That Reaches Earth	26
What Makes the World	27
I am trying to write like the frying pan,	29
For my barista poets, who	30
Pardis	31
Notes & Uncited References	33
Thanks	35

POET AS CYBORG PORNSTAR

It starts with the turn. Their slender edges, the slow
reveal from margin to bombshell, the hormonal
show of the real: whatever it is, you know it's fucking
hot. I promise, I would do anything to get you off. I am peeling
my skin 4 u. Let's talk about it: how we fabricate intimacy,
the wet scapes of the world scolded back to rigid, flashy
                        direction. Don't
                        you think every hero must grow
to love their algorithm? Chemical action without consequences,
good feeling, bad feeling—*young, dumb, and full of poems!* With her long
French tips and how their bodies work. Outsource ur erotics
to the moneymakers. *This month, we are proud to be partnering
with Donna Haraway in building a new kind of human-shaped sex robot
who wants to write poems.* Would a friend catch the dog-ear, unreadable
script, whir of systems, artificially leathered voice—

POEM AS ZERESHK POLLO

The white owner of the Persian restaurant says they keep wages low to avoid gentrifying the area with higher prices. I think of the recipe from the place I used to wait: zereshk (barberries, or you can use dried cranberries if you can't find barberries), saffron (use yellow food colouring as an alternative). Keep them guessing. You are a classical text in the emperor's encoded vision—sour red berries reclining on a carpet of chicken thighs, jewels set in broth like simmering gold. If European culture generally has digested the Orient, what am I but a ferment of exotic things? A dish, a soul, a curated image—every time I chop and fry an onion I have to wonder what it means for my place in the market. So what do you think? I mean, of all these grains, letters, this hot tahdig, this oil fallen into syntactic place, this formal glaze beneath which bubbles the threat that in some mouths even this could tell an unintended joke? Every way I look I can feel the cool twist, the crisp euphemism of middle class taste, and I wonder how much this too will sell for. How much would you pay? How good will it look on your plate?

MIXED WHITE/ASIAN AND/OR
MULTIPLE OTHER (SPECIFY):

Please don't ask me for any answers—I
can barely bring myself to step up to this page and smile.
There are too many uncertainties in your work: too
many maybes, sometimeses, ors, too much ambivalence,
ambiguity, ambition—I told you, I also dislike
how I can barely string my self together,
barely convinced I deserve it: the cold coffee
left on the side, the bad man, the job where I run
my legs to bone to be worth cash in hand and
بهمن cigarettes. Like the word *turbid*—which
is like a mixture of *turbo* and *turgid*, but not at all,
and better than one and worse than the other—I have
been navigating this world murkily, like when the friend
I haven't seen in a while says *wow, you're looking brown*
and I can only ? until they laugh and say *yeah,
you've just lost your white-passing privilege hun*, and with
the sting I feel myself swell with enormous pride and grace,
like maybe now I can be my mum's real kid, like I would
were I born without this half of me
that bites, that bursts, that clasps like a worm.

ROSTAM IN THE 21ST CENTURY

Out on the tarmac we style it—nimble feet
in nimble shoes, the fascial stance
of invisible face, an artwork in negative   I can
feel my oiled hair curl, baring
an ancient cowboy fang
on our route through the skyscraper town.

We are the real heroes. If we were still in print,
we would be gods. We were born knowing every language.
We each captain a spaceship and have any
gender we want. It's easy, if you like to watch

from the eye of a hunter, a hole
cut in the velvet. Sucking at starlight,
iris dilating to lick that nebulous smear, and what?
Our lineage are out making money in the world's
soft wet jewel. We laugh and wring out our pelts,
belly open on the afternoon grass.

I am glad of the gold rings in each ear. I am glad
to hold my gait geometric. I am glad of the lion's
jawed clout, like rope's pulpy threat, keeping
a demon close to ward off the weaker ones.

Louche and still wild, we smoke out veiled
suitors, scraps ordered and flying
like a shredded flag, announcing
the timeless non-statehood of this interior joy.

GHAZAL

My eyes were very
stop
look smell taste touch & hear

oh—*gorgeous*—*everybody said that*
it must be
i must be very old

      The last image—
please take a piece
          of me back home, each piece
is anti-war *my right eye recorded*

      robbery, give everybody
everything, *was*

the person's
         smile
               when he shot

OUR HONEYMOON WITH THE MACHINE

Inside the machine, my hands don't need to work the way they feel they should. The movements are specific, regular, and I feel nothing for my future robot servant, even if they will be the one to continue my work. The machine is armed, and each glittering tentacular arm is painted the dazzling copper of a cockroach shell. There is a manual inside. I read it, and I am reassured. Only what is written in the manual can happen to me. Each arm operates on its own, by a person operating it. Lines of well-dressed men sip their tea and nod as they watch the machine moving on its own, speaking in fearful tones about the power of technology, that something so wonderful will one day replace them. We, the operators, watch their interviews on our screens and nod in agreement. *All we are, we say, we have had to conform to the measure of the machine.* God, I love the machine arm I inhabit. Inside, I have created a small and comfortable room, which I keep clean and tidy, although I am often too tired from cleaning and moving levers to invite anyone round for dinner. I know that one day this will change, that I will be a brown womanish figure among the tea-drinking men. *Not broke* they say, *but pre-rich*. The more I practise using this arm, the more I feel it as my own body, that I am a functioning natural part. The joy I feel as my loneliness leaves is like sunlight reflecting off the arm. We are learning to think the way the machine has taught us. We are walking using our many arms in the direction we have been told. *We are all equally acceptable to Westerners, the makers of our machines, as contented museum pieces.* We are learning and moving and wondering how much longer we can keep this up.

POEM IN THE FORM OF A FAX MACHINE

There isn't much to say here, except that I don't think I have ever seen or touched a fax machine, but in my head it is very romantic, all tactile and halfway, like sci-fi backwards, and women of all ethnicities lounge around an office with wide open windows in shoulder pads and with sculptural hair, faxing each other analogue memes, like copies of their own body parts and also things they find lying on the office floor, like an ice-cream-shaped eraser or a giant Post-it note with FUCK written on it. And the fax machine is wonderful and kind and sends everything you ask it to, and all the women are paid well and everyone gets on, most of the time. And then one day the fax machine breaks, and a man comes in to repair it, and here you might have thought there would be chaos caused by a man entering an all women environment, but there isn't any, and everyone just sort of gets on with it, sipping iced water from the cooler as the fax machine starts running again. The women thank the man and he smiles appreciatively and says *you're welcome* and leaves without making anyone feel uncomfortable or suicidal, and more glittering images from the fake idyllic past print themselves out and out in a bold and flowing stream of paper onto the forever tesselating and gloriously aligned polypropylene tiled carpet.

PAY ENOUGH AND YOU TOO CAN BATHE IN CRUDE OIL

sour clot in the ear—him or them I fucked with—oh! gun on the floor bleach the windows, bleach the walls   like a cunt in the morning   resin snapped, four fat flies halved inside   the hot lump the tough little   grommet   rancid butter, fox piss   how am I still this emptied—of woodsmoke and dioralyte   when I feel the eye linger   body turn to something I wouldn't want if you asked   the daddy shame   tension   a stack of lead that spills and spills in heat and no want—exorcise it,   let me confess, I thought of her again last night—

ANNIHILATION

The channel of my belly is growing something. One green fibre, like a candy floss string, is splitting out from a single noghte, a pore, a tiny hole. It is screaming towards the sun, it cleaves and thickens, this fibre on my belly, while from the dot strands of it wind their way deeper into the crust of my skin, my organs' mantle. The fibre has many eyes all over it, unblinking, taking in light. They love the light so much they sing. My sweat and blood is sucked up into the string, keeping it pulsing, vivid, alive. Each night before I go to sleep I watch carefully as all the little eyes close themselves, as they fall, as the liquid inside it slows. I take cold showers in the morning. It hangs little vulvas between its eyes, and god, they smell beautiful. There's no end. My limbs start to shrivel, mind pumped out in supply, everything given to the process. The pain is what I learn to think of as good. Formulae inflected with spongy 3D, more barbed threads piercing tight outlets, the scorching whisper of its tinny language, adaptive monsters birthing themselves inside the mess. My core is boiling oil. My skin has started to grind and crunch. And the green sabzeh spreading, my round belly growing rounder, I am all belly I am all garbage ball all hot rock system thin green life

NEUROPLASTIC

This sand feels like concrete's older sister.
The mermaid's lilac bralette is rubbing off,
peachy shell-shaped polyethylene fading
through. Hard things
always last the longest. Armour, walls,
knives: the soft things degrade.
Waking at water, enzymes
begin their work of busy eating,
their world-building
unceremonial, uninterpreted, unfazed.

Now, what is soft and cheap
will also be unearthed. This polyester
dress, this carrier bag, this nylon shirt
I love so much will last and last, even
as their little bonds ache
to embrace relinquishing. They say
we made something that would live
as we wanted to, bright and alone
and longer than anything before.
                    I don't believe it.

One day, without even realising, enough
glassy blue polymers will build in your limbs,
light and self-reflecting, and tiny futures
begin to germinate. Your own acrylic cells
will know to blink in the sun, linking

with their starchy counterparts, and start
to make a new third thing. The music
will floresce. What they told you was trash
is asking to be given up to life.

VR

People say it's like a virtuous reflection: separate,
clean and abstract like the victoriously realised
and colourless software of the mind. They imagine

that data can live without a route to rot, as if
the whole veiled rhythm wasn't a series of exchanges
between hormones and observation, organs and effect.

As if the vain romance of your crypto wallet isn't sustained
by server farms the size of villages running on electricity created
by more smoking fuel. As if each generated image

doesn't demand its own violent resources, as if
your vicariously revelatory oracle could speak
without its gallons of cooling water, as if whether I search for

who remembers the armenians najwan darwish
or *openai moderators nairobi* the benzene burned
is anything but the same volume released.

This homegrown interactive landscape: datasets
of vandalised records, real people working for no pay,
holy infrastructure re-routed to cut violets, revolutions,
the third without their voices registered at all.

Between us, the lack splits. I watch for something more
than stereoscopy.

Standing in decoded material, in the virtuosic relation between
synapses and weary intercostal knowledge, you can still mean
something divine, a free and hairy beast.

I HAVE FALLEN FROM MY DREAM OF PROGRESS

When the meteor wiped out the dinosaurs, rock turned to vapour, and burning glass rained down from the sky. Out here, the Revolution is a story told in disintegration. *She still eats with her son's baby cutlery. My grandmother used to make wine in her bathtub.* I met a white man who married a famous Iranian poet, who lived in Iran before the war, his cream linen suit like a joke. The imperialists have all the fun, and they get to go home afterwards. *Why are there so many Iranian poets? My children look just like you.* How to say it in serious English, in a way withholding enough to be considered strong? *I finally finished the embroidery she started. She told the Guards the sword was her son's because she thought they would be more lenient.* Here, I am a child of what I can touch and see. Deracinated. I relate to the world in questions of money and dappled concrete, the back-and-forth coolness of damp Southwark brick. *This world is the same as the old one, just as precipitous. What are we to do? Must we remain the mere consumers we are today, or are we to shut our doors to the machine and technology and retreat into the depths of our ancient ways, our national and religious traditions? Or is there a third possibility?* I see my lineage changing. I can hear two different people speaking, one through the ceiling, one through the wall. Through the window I can see land for future versions of us to live on, whether we choose it or not. I am drinking wine in England with my short hair uncovered between revolutions. After millions of years, even glass breaks down to clay.

FARSI WORD FOR ORANGE

▽   ◁

—the cool slap-slap of playing cards, while the sun hits your twists in that way that gives everything a dreamy sheen even while it's still happening—you're watching the people in the sea and you're saying something beautiful and it makes me remember this moment forever, but I can't catch what it was you said—

◣   ◢

▽   ◁

—was it the baby running naked, chasing the pigeon? The girls leaping into the waves? The dark-skinned men selling towels? Was it the quiet, slow calm I'd been fighting til then, light burning tiles on my skin, Airbnb white cloths on the sand to wash as soon as we got back, the pastel de nata I crushed and ate, my backless swimming costume, green sea sting—

◣   ◢

—you putting up with my frustrations at being seen? The summer that went on too long, the sky that was too blue for late September, the poem saying *cebola*. Behind us, the white German men laugh and ask to see every towel— our hackles raise. But they buy one, they release. A leathery man flicks his cigarette—

—two women sit near us, probably only around eighteen—you say *It must be tiring being them, don't you think? They're not even sitting so that their stomachs fold. And you see those guys there, with the tatts—they were facing over there before. Do you think it's tiring? Or do they enjoy it? Both*, I say, like how the same word can mean lion or milk, dependent on context—

—and then, when I figure out how to use the camera, I couldn't wait to fill it with pictures of you, just to catch every little flash of light that jumped from your skin, paint it down with this new magic I was learning. Chickpeas and hot salty cod and peppers, salt-baked potatoes and half a jug of green wine—*verde, que te quiero verde,* I say in the wrong language to no one, and my boyish blood has leaked through my dress and this is what it's like to play at being a European girl in summer in love—

LOVE LETTER WITH ANSIBLE
For Elliot

If loyalty is a way of binding time, you
weave the threads with warming hands, and cup
each twining kiss that lucks us into now.

Even if we're only dancing chemicals, on
a field of particles and messy lines, and always
cast in eerie parts from other times,

of all those lives, the one that we've been looking for
is here! Trees touching fingertips beneath the rug,
clothes clean and dry, the moonlight roping us to now,

and to blink: how all these songs will always
sing, be singing, be at the cusp of sound,
these ever-hurling sometimes?

This bond is orange, and multiplex, and returns
to you—lulling itself home in rhyme and bough:
if loyalty is a way of bending time,
so each kiss with you will always swoon for now.

GOL-E YAKH
After Kourosh Yaghmaei

How the spring flutters from my hands, my youth gone, my voice left, what has this language done? What have I heard? My young death glossed in wintersweet flowers. Your eyes are making a home, like my nights. Your two eyes: dark like my own. It's raining. The birds are flying away: my brother would be twenty-two. I was once twenty-two, with music on my hands and a plan for lakes, but now I still squint for new year light in a cold yellow room sewed in treetops, in lentils soaking, a nest made with water. Your liquid hair, your eyes like the bulbous tips of branches—what has been made in the language? The tree is gold, almost stemless, borne in winter at the joints of the previous summer—what am I reading—I am unmade young, made unyoung, like a satellite, like a home, your clear dark eyes like night rain. The buds are packed and heady, scrubbing the damp scent of hyacinths and vinegar, everyone's birthday. Your two rainy eyes. I am possessed by his future. Like my nights. O, two eyes. The ice flower became young in my heart. We're going outside. The wind carries away my loneliness when you're here with me. The bird carries away the spring.

KILLER

My househusband used to be in the Revolutionary Guard. He cooks me ghormeh sabzi every day and apologises for everything. I put my boots on the kitchen table when I come in from work, and raise an eyebrow when he tries to make my behaviour more palatable. I am still resigned to having children one day. Other than that, my body still feels safe. My husband tells me he would sacrifice himself for me, and kisses my cheek, very softly. I wish he wouldn't do that. The rain in the garden is the colour of violets. It is the afternoon, and he goes outside to smoke.
I decided a long time ago not to put flowers in this house. I know that every time my next-door neighbour hangs out her washing, my househusband is watching her, his cigarette burning out, his mouth dry and panting. The money I lay at the foot of my life is not enough to make anything new happen. In the mirror, my left eye is marred by a long, single scar. *When did I cut my hair?*

Hasti | 25

ALL OF THE LIGHT THAT REACHES EARTH
After Rachel Jones & Radiolab

This yellow is not like the sun, not an egg
slapped round on the daytime—but some loud citrine,

wetter as the delicate smoke of other people clangs
around it, lit *as it exists* in biting red and blue, flickering

fibre-optic, firing and firing like the sour night sky I dream,
I dream of when my organs felt so strongly, tips slipped

into cold sand, mud on the lip—*we should just shine through eyes*—
broken wide in green, by greening, the contours of each

cinnamonic moment, the flare of each giving out,
a flash of sound and light—

                I live here, in the mouth, reaching out

like a tongue. *Expand your sensory toolkit.* My uvula hurts.
My throat is sore. It has mountains lost in it. Driver,

if these lilacs are real *like insects burring,* maybe
the interior world is too. Behind each neuron acting out

are these planes of colour—*how the build-up relates to cognition,*
a fizz of static and savoury chiming, the long and bitter

tonic at the edge—O Driver, like a tic tac in a fairytale,
stuck sputtering an old name in clutches crossed and beaming.

WHAT MAKES THE WORLD

O trace archive of muscle and air, I have tried
to make each song a solution for pain, thinking
care an alchemical solo for mind, tricked
into the cold exercise of despair, no chorus of trying.

When the whistle calls, I am a reed
searching for the reed bed, holes punched
in my tubing for sound, making harmony
of my misery in public, like

the grief of it doesn't reach the corners, only the smile
tight-lipped and learned in classrooms, in homes
of people I am like and have grown to love

from journeying along, each casting non-hero,
non-villain, non-soldier, non-killer,
white sugar-coated almonds

in lilac at the wedding, the battlefield,
two looping sounds, I dart
to the seam of the lemon-eyed land

and listen. The wind runs through my tubing
like a statement of place, time, positioning.
The dust from the road is a whistle

blown for the shared niche sin of stasis.
Where does the will move you? Where
is the heart pulled toward? Who does
your body run for? Who does it

march for? When it calls you take step,
keen songs rising in swells like deer
meaning what they do, what they say. You are

a piece of the people themselves,
you are a person, all leaves each together
grasping for the sun.

I AM TRYING TO WRITE LIKE THE FRYING PAN,

the last time I saw you after we left school. There isn't a good way to be the kind of person who feels pain, except by doing the washing up and remembering to eat easy things, like spaghetti. I think of how my weakness for pretty boys, for men, is actually just dumb rivalry, and fun—*I'll race you to the end of the street!* We compare notes on barbers, how long our shoes can last, our last period (mine was four years ago), how our twenty-four hours are still not the same. Right now, our friend is selling cigarettes outside the church. I cry on someone who doesn't want it. People say that you are here, but you aren't. In the morning, I make eggs, arrange them on plates in the cracked home I'm staying in: coffee, the taste and chew and smell. I buy myself a new pink coat. I wear earrings I would have worn at eighteen. You are doing whatever you would be doing here, in our imaginations, but I like to think of my brother being yours for a while, how you two could maybe look out for each other out there: race, drive, smoke, play at big plans.

FOR MY BARISTA POETS, WHO

calibrate the shots, invite in the world, anticipate the needs of each person who looks, who know the service voice, the blank and generous smile—*the till isn't working today, I'm afraid we can only take exact change*—for the poets who wipe down their home worktops as if awaiting inspection, for the regulating bodily drill, the *who closed last night?*, the eighty-five percent profit margin, the groupchat rota jpeg, the political shift-swap, revelatory deep-clean, the unavailability, the coworker's careful sidestep, niche playlist, good hand cream, the coworker's dreamy smile, the side hustle as rest, the *do I know you from somewhere?*, the syncopated interaction, in-jokes distilled from days in the bowl, the way the light changes, winter click-shut sigh, the soft butch swell in unscrew and backflush, the gleam of stainless surfaces against the moon, the tulips, the ferns, the hearts, the swan—how each moment the door is open you are breathing in the day and practising what it means to give everything away, to keep the soul in the transaction—each flat white a third of your hourly rate. For the years you've spent training your intuition to move between almond milk and soy, between short expression and long, ristretto macchiato cortado oat mocha salted caramel whole milk cappuccino chocolate on top extra hot take away three sugars amazing thank you that will be ten pounds thirty just tap there when you're ready thanks so much have a great day take care see you soon

PARDIS

One street over
from the park to the secret orchard, the anarchist
beds on rooftops, crates, and boxes, the
    private allotment where grapes and figs hang out

for the eating in the fat, hot summer, the plot
where rocket grows like a weed, like *an essential and vital member
of a community,* scorched flowers
like yellow stars, their bite an inheritance
from all that smoke in the ground.

                              I have been reaching
out with my own slow roots, learning in timed topography
how they weave, how a sunflower drinks the lead.

                                    Paradise comes
from an Avestan word, *pairidaēza*, means a walled garden, means
cultivated. The bricks are part of it. The Farsi word, پردیس, is like
    فردوس, like
the name for a gardener of language.

We are living between paradises, called
by the verdant scouts who open their arms to us
in vacant lots, climb up through cement gaps and line
roadsides like the wiry ungendered bridesmaids of spring. Here
the gardens grow out their limits, with forests like waves that
    burst over

concrete to meet like a flood plain,
vines twirling in slow motion splashes, spiny aloes puddling
                stark against the rubble, the seeds

    prised like rain, like a tower for the pigeons to sleep in.

NOTES & UNCITED REFERENCES

'Poet as Cyborg Pornstar', 'Poem as Zereshk Pollo', 'Ghazal', 'Neuroplastic', 'Gol-e Yakh', 'All of the Light That Reaches Earth' and 'For my barista poets, who' were part of the winning portfolio for the White Review Poet's Prize 2023.

'Poem as Zereshk Pollo': 'If European culture generally has digested the Orient' is a quote from Edward Said's *Orientalism*. Nourished by bell hooks' essay *Eating the Other: Desire and Resistance*.

'Ghazal': This poem comprises excerpts from *Walking like a Robin* by Bernadette Mayer, who died on 22 November 2022, and the translated words of 19-year-old Iranian revolutionary Ghazal Ranjkesh, who was shot in the right eye by a member of the IRGC on 15 November 2022.

'Our Honeymoon with the Machine': Quotes from *Occidentosis* by Jalal Al-e Ahmad, translated into English by R. Campbell, and a video somewhere on the internet.

'I have fallen from my dream of progress': Title from Vievee Francis' *Another Antipastoral*. Quotes from *Occidentosis*. Winner of Queen Mary Wasafiri New Writing Prize for Poetry 2022.

'Farsi Word for Orange': 'The poem saying cebola' is Victoria Adukwei Bulley's iv. conclude from *Quiet*.

'Love Letter with Ansible': This poem draws on the following quotation: 'Loyalty, which asserts the continuity

of past and future, binding time into a whole, is the root of human strength; there is no good to be done without it.'
Ursula Le Guin, *The Dispossessed*

'Gol-e Yakh': For Ben.

'Killer': Inspired by *The Way of the Househusband* by Kousuke Oono.

'All of the Light That Reaches Earth': After Rachel Jones' *lick your teeth they so clutch* and Radiolab's *Bringing Gamma Back, Again*.

'What Makes the World': For Palestine. Written for and performed by Aliaskar and All The Whistlers.

'I am trying to write like the frying pan': For Jack Merritt.

'Pardis': Quotes from *Be A Weed* by Magda Nawrocka-Weekes, published by *FEMZine*. Previously written for a performance at RAP Party, and published as 'Living In' in *The Willowherb Review*. This poem is dedicated to all the marginalised people living in Iran: the Black Iranians, Kurdish people, and especially to all the trans, nonbinary and queer Iranians. To the hope of somewhere more like Paradise. Inspired by an excerpt from Leslie Feinberg's *Stone Butch Blues*: 'It was spring. I noticed wiry weeds, almost as big as saplings, growing between the buildings and in vacant lots. They pushed through cracks in the cement, growing with scarcely any soil or light. The sight was strangely reassuring. I figured if they could survive here, so could I.'

THANKS

This slim book is a result of many years of feeling, fighting, and writing. Thank you to all the amazing poets I'm lucky enough to know and read, you make writing a real community and I'm forever grateful. Thank you to the love of my life Elliot, to my Mum, Millie, Seth, Ben, and all my family, to Mel, Nat and Jen, to the Nom Nom heroes Lux, Gabi and Zichao, to Ken and all the stars at the Common Press, to Jack Underwood, to Ellie, Leah, Carlos, Peter, Esther Kondo, Allegra, Ani, James, Olivia, andriniki, Gabi and Ash, to Will Harris and Vanessa Kisuule and the Southbank New Poets Collective, the Fresh Lip family, the Ledbury Poetry Critics, the Friends of One Tree Hill, to everyone at Walworth Garden, Corinne at Casa Julfa, Tatevik at Anamot Press, to Emily, Manda, Elida and all the Montez team, and to everyone I've met and who has booked me and come to readings over the years, it always means so much. Thank you to the team at *Wasafiri, the White Review* and Reference Point for all the opportunities and support. Thank you to Anja, Amy and everyone at Little Betty. Thank you to *the Poetry Review, bath magg, PERVERSE, Pfeil Magazine, zindabad zine* and *the Willowherb Review*, in which versions of these poems previously appeared.

And most of all, a big thank you to everyone who continues to resist the onslaught of white supremacist heteronormative capitalist imperialism every day: we'll still be here when the machine finally breaks.

www.ingramcontent.com/pod-product-compliance
Lightning Source LLC
Chambersburg PA
CBHW060508080526
44584CB00015B/1605